Filled
With
the Spirit

Filled With the Spirit

WHAT THE SCRIPTURES SAY ABOUT THE PENTECOSTAL BAPTISM

ROBERT C. CUNNINGHAM

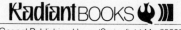

RadiantBOOKS

Gospel Publishing House/Springfield. Mo. 65802

02-0712

FILLED WITH THE SPIRIT
© 1972 by the
Gospel Publishing House
Springfield, Missouri 65802

ISBN 0-88243-712-7

Library of Congress Catalog Card Number 73-190446

Printed in the United States of America

Contents

Chapter One

What Does It Mean?

TO BE FILLED with the Spirit is to experience that which 120 disciples of the Lord Jesus Christ experienced when "they were all filled with the Holy Ghost, and began to speak with other tongues, as the Spirit gave them utterance" (Acts 2:4).

This experience is often called the baptism of the Spirit, because Jesus had described it in terms of a baptism. So had John the Baptist.

As much as three years earlier, John had said, "I indeed baptize you with water unto repentance: but he that cometh after me is mightier than I, whose shoes I am not worthy to bear: he shall baptize you with the Holy Ghost, and with fire" (Matthew 3:11).

Jesus had mentioned it just before He departed and ascended into heaven. "John truly baptized with water," He said, "but ye shall be baptized with the Holy Ghost not many days hence" (Acts 1:5).

A GIFT FROM HEAVEN

The great event took place in an upper

room in Jerusalem, the Bible says (Acts 1:13). It is described in Acts 2:1-4, as follows:

"And when the day of Pentecost was fully come, they were all with one accord in one place.

"And suddenly there came a sound from heaven as of a rushing mighty wind, and it filled all the house where they were sitting.

"And there appeared unto them cloven tongues like as of fire, and it sat upon each of them.

"And they were all filled with the Holy Ghost, and began to speak with other tongues, as the Spirit gave them utterance."

According to Acts 1:14, 15, there were both men and women in that group of 120 disciples and the Spirit came upon them all. The Bible says the noise of those 120 persons magnifying God in various languages, together with the sound of that marvelous wind from heaven, was so loud it attracted a huge crowd. "What meaneth this?" asked these spectators. The apostle Peter explained the strange happening by saying that Jesus had poured the Spirit upon them in fulfillment of the prophecy recorded in Joel 2:28.

Peter said: "Therefore being by the right hand of God exalted, and having received of the Father the promise of the Holy Ghost, he hath shed forth this, which ye now see and hear" (Acts 2:33).

He then told all the onlookers that if they would repent and be baptized in the name of Jesus Christ, every one of them also would receive this same wonderful gift of the Holy Spirit (Acts 2:38).

If you have not yet been baptized with the Holy Ghost, this booklet is written to help you understand what the Scriptures teach on the subject and to encourage you to receive this exhilarating, empowering experience for yourself.

THE NEW TESTAMENT STANDARD

Notice that, although Jesus had said in Acts 1:5 that the disciples would be *"baptized* with the Holy Ghost," Acts 2:4 states they were *"filled* with the Holy Ghost." Evidently the terms "baptized" and "filled" are interchangeable in this case. When one is "baptized" with the Spirit he is "filled" with the Spirit, like a cup that is filled to the point of overflowing, or a sponge that is saturated in every part.

This is the New Testament standard for every Christian believer. God wants each of us to be filled to capacity with His Holy Spirit so that our minds, our affections, our spirits, and our bodies are completely impregnated, possessed, and controlled by Him.

By observing other terms used concerning the Spirit we may learn more about what it means to be baptized with the Holy Ghost.

RIVERS OF LIVING WATER

Jesus said, "He that believeth on me, as the scripture hath said, out of his belly shall flow *rivers of living water.* (But this spake he of the Spirit, which they that believe on him should receive: for the Holy Ghost was not yet given; because that Jesus was not yet glorified)" (John 7:38, 39). Notice, in passing, how the terms "the Spirit" and "the Holy Ghost" are used synonymously in verse 39. There is no difference between "the Holy Spirit" and "the Holy Ghost." Modern translators prefer the former term simply because it is more understandable. This is permissible, as the Greek text makes no distinction.

The striking point here is the parallel Jesus draws between the Holy Spirit and flowing rivers. To be filled with the Spirit is to have "rivers of living water" flowing from one's inmost being. What a tremendous ministry this opens up to everyone. Even those who may have considered themselves unimportant, with few talents, can do a significant work for God! Jesus said, "He that believeth on me. . . ." The weakest, most obscure men and women can have this experience by believing on Jesus. Whatever their occupation, wherever they are—whether at home, in an office, at a factory, whatever their circumstances—if they believe on Jesus they may receive the Holy Spirit and have "rivers of living water" flowing from within.

Jesus used the word "rivers." Do not be satisfied with a cupful when the Lord offers rivers. The invitation is, "If any man thirst, let him come unto me, and drink" (John 7:37). You can have all you want. He gives the Spirit without reservation to those who are thirsty enough to drink, and drink, and keep drinking until they are filled to overflowing.

THE PROMISE OF THE FATHER

Here is another interesting name for the Holy Spirit baptism. Jesus told His disciples not to depart from Jerusalem but to "wait for *the promise of the Father*" (Acts 1:4). We have many promises from our Heavenly Father, but only one is called *"the* promise." In the next verse Jesus explained what it means. "Wait for the promise of the Father, which, saith he, ye have heard of me. For John truly baptized with water; but ye shall be baptized with the Holy Ghost...."

After His ascension, Jesus "received of the Father the promise of the Holy Ghost" (Acts 2:33).

Paul said the blessing of Abraham had come on the Gentiles through Jesus Christ "that we might receive the promise of the Spirit through faith" (Galatians 3:14).

Jesus said, "Behold, I send the promise of my Father upon you" (Luke 24:49). To whom does "the promise" belong? It belongs to all the Father's children without distinction or favor.

Peter, when he answered the onlookers on the Day of Pentecost, declared to them, "The promise is unto you, and to your children, and to all that are afar off, even as many as the Lord our God shall call" (Acts 2:39).

Therefore it is for you. It is like a check made out to you, waiting to be cashed; or a promissory note, waiting to be honored. God wants you to present your claim and receive this glorious experience.

Other Terms Used

The gift. Peter spoke of receiving "the *gift* of the Holy Ghost" (Acts 2:38). Jesus also called it a gift, saying, "If ye then, being evil, know how to *give good gifts* unto your children: how much more shall your Heavenly Father *give* the Holy Spirit to them that ask him?" (Luke 11:1).

Receiving. When the apostles laid their hands on the Samaritan converts, "they *received* the Holy Ghost" (Acts 8:17). Again, when Paul arrived at Ephesus he asked the disciples there, "Have ye *received* the Holy Ghost since ye believed?" (Acts 19:2). Receiving is a distinct, deliberate act on our part. Although the Holy Spirit is a gift, we are not benefitted until we "receive," appropriate, and accept the gift.

Pouring out. God said, "I will *pour out* of my Spirit upon all flesh" (Acts 2:17). The Bible speaks of the Spirit being *"shed forth"* on the Day of Pentecost (Acts 2:33) and *"poured out"* at Caesarea (Acts 10:45). This comparison to a downpour emphasizes God's willingness to give us the Spirit in copious measure.

Falling. The apostles prayed that the Samaritans might receive the Holy Ghost, "for as yet he was *fallen* upon none of them" (Acts 8:16). We read also how "the Holy Ghost *fell*" on the people of Cornelius' household (Acts 10:44). This term suggests how suddenly—and even unexpectedly, perhaps—the blessing may come sometimes. For His own good reasons God may bestow the Spirit upon one supplicant immediately, and let another supplicant wait a little while; but let us remember that His delays are not denials. He will give us the Spirit as soon as we are prepared to receive Him.

Coming. Acts 19:6 states "the Holy Ghost *came* on them." The same expression is used in John 15:26; 16:7, 8, 13; and Acts 1:8. *The reference denotes personality.* The Holy Ghost is not merely an influence, as some suppose. He is a Person, just as Christ is a Person (for there are three Persons in the Godhead —Father, Son, and Holy Ghost). It is written that "Christ Jesus *came* into the world..." (1 Timothy 1:15). Similarly, it is written that "the Holy Ghost *came* on them." The Holy Ghost should never be called "it." The Authorized Version erroneously speaks of "the Spirit itself" in Romans 8:16 and 26. The personal pronoun is indicated in the Greek text, so the correct translation is, "The Spirit Himself."

Sealed. Paul made the statement, "After that ye believed, ye were *sealed* with that holy Spirit of promise" (Ephesians 1:13). He also stated that God has "*sealed* us, and given the earnest of the Spirit in our hearts" (2 Corinthians 1:22). The "sealing" refers to their being baptized with the Holy Ghost, for both the Ephesians and the Corinthians had received this experience. The "sealing" of Ephesians 1:13 is the "receiving" of Acts 19:2 and the "coming on them" of Acts 19:6.

Notice the successive stages through which these believers passed, as indicated in Ephesians 1:13. (1) There was a time when they were pagans, living in heathen darkness. (2) Then they received light through the preaching of the gospel. (3) They accepted the light and were saved—"In whom ye also trusted, after that ye heard the word of truth, the gospel of your salvation." (4) *After* this, they were sealed—"In whom also *after* that ye believed, ye were sealed with that holy Spirit of promise." This is the normal course of Christian experience according to the New Testament. We repent of our sins, receive the Lord Jesus as our personal Saviour, dedicate our lives to Him, and then we are baptized with the Holy Ghost to make us effective witnesses for Christ.

POWER FOR WITNESSING

The great purpose of being baptized with the Holy Ghost was described by the Lord Jesus when He said, "Ye shall receive power, after that the Holy Ghost is come upon you: and ye shall be witnesses unto me. . . ." (Acts 1:8). The Spirit gives us power to witness forcefully and effectively.

One man, after being filled with the Spirit, told what a change came in his life. "Prayer and worship, which before had been so much a matter of effort and duty, now became the breath of life to me," he said. "Talking about Jesus to others became the most natural thing in the world. Now that He was so wonderfully real to me, it was much easier to make Him real to others."

This is what the Spirit does—He makes Jesus

so real and wonderful. Jesus said, "When he, the Spirit of truth, is come ... he shall glorify me: for he shall receive of mine, and shall show it unto you" (John 16:13, 14).

One new Pentecostal testified: "I sometimes wonder what we talked about and what we did with ourselves before we were filled with the Holy Spirit. The love of Christ seems to fill my whole life now, and I find myself wanting to share Him with practically everybody."

Another described how his prayer life was revolutionized. He said: "I had been born of the Spirit, but that night I was filled with the Spirit. By faith I had known that I was His, but He came in and took possession. Up to that moment *I* had been praying. But now *He* had come in and was praying through me with a power, a faith, and intensity entirely different and so much more wonderful than my own. In experience I was now the temple of the Holy Ghost."

POWER FOR PRAYING

This revolutionary power in prayer is one great reason why we need the Spirit. In Jude 20 we are told to be "praying in the Holy Ghost." When we are filled with the Spirit we can pray in the Spirit, and God can direct our praying. In ourselves we know not what we should pray for, but the Spirit knows; and when He has control of our lives, He is able to pray through us in harmony with the will of God (Romans 8:26).

The Spirit would not be given if we did not need Him. The fact is that without His gracious presence and power we cannot serve God effectively. Today as truly as in Zerubbabel's day, it is "not by might, nor by power, but by my Spirit, saith the Lord of hosts" (Zechariah 4:6).

Human strength—whether physical, mental, or moral—is never sufficient to accomplish God's purposes on earth. We cannot serve God effectively in our own power, and the Lord does not expect us to try. He wants us to be filled with the Spirit so He may do His work through us.

A COMMAND TO BE OBEYED

Evangelist Billy Graham tells of preaching one Sunday morning in a certain church which had a problem. The problem was a deacon who came to church drunk!

"The church had a congregational meeting," said Dr. Graham, "and excommunicated him. They should have.

"I asked the pastor, 'Does every deacon come every Sunday filled with the Holy Spirit?' He said, 'No.'

"I said, 'Did you ever kick them out for this offense?' He said, 'No.'

"I said, 'Why not? The same Scripture that says, "Be not drunk with wine," also says, "Be filled with the Spirit." ' "

Some seem to view the fullness of the Holy Spirit as a luxury, rather than a necessity. They consider the experience desirable, but optional.

The Bible, however, makes it mandatory. Jesus *commanded* His disciples not to depart

from Jerusalem until they had been filled
with the Holy Spirit (Acts 1:4, 5). Paul used
imperative language when he said, "Be filled
with the Spirit" (Ephesians 5:18). It is a command we must obey.

Chapter Two

What Must One Do to Experience It?

WE HAVE SEEN THAT to be baptized with the Holy Ghost is (1) a promise to be claimed, (2) a gift to be received, and (3) a command to be obeyed. The question before us now is, *What should a person do in order to receive this experience?*

The answer, in its simplest form, is just this: *ask God for it.* Jesus said the Father will "give the Holy Spirit to them that *ask* him" (Luke 11:13).

SEEK WITH ALL YOUR HEART

Halfhearted seekers will never receive the blessing, for the Lord said, "Ye shall seek me, and find me, when ye shall search for me with all your heart" (Jeremiah 29:13).

Neither will doubters. God demands unwavering faith on the part of those who ask Him for the Spirit. James 1:6, 7 says, "Let him ask in faith, nothing wavering. For he that wavereth is like a wave of the sea driven with the wind and tossed. For let not that man think that he shall receive any thing of the Lord."

A firm faith and a great sense of need are prime requisites for receiving the Holy Spirit.

ADMIT YOU ARE WEAK

Human nature likes to feel self-sufficient, but our natural strength cannot cope with the demands of the Christian life. We need spiritual power for spiritual living, and the only Source of that power is the Spirit of God.

S. D. Gordon, a great Baptist preacher, said many years ago: "There is one inlet of power in the life—anybody's life—any kind of power; just one inlet—the Holy Spirit." We need the Spirit's fullness, not merely for power to preach or work miracles, but for day-by-day living.

A British minister, Walter Urch, has pointed out that the Greek word *dunamis* appears no less than 121 times in the New Testament.

In many cases this Greek word is translated "power," reminding us of an explosive force (the word dynamite is derived from *dunamis*). For example, the Lord told His disciples they would be endued with power (*dunamis*) from on high (Luke 24:49). Later He explained this would follow the coming of the Holy Spirit upon them (Acts 1:8). They did indeed receive a spiritual force that was dynamic in its effects, for it exploded in miracles of salvation, healing, and other mighty exploits to advance the cause of Christ.

But this same word *dunamis* has been translated in less spectacular terms also, including ability, virtue, and abundance. In 2 Corinthians 12:9, 10, it is translated "strength." We are given a picture of the apostle Paul, weak in body, poor and persecuted, yet resolutely pursuing his God-appointed ministry. Where did he obtain this ability to suffer, endure, and persevere? He found it not in himself, but in the power (*dunamis*) of Christ. Surely all of us need this power of endurance, and we may have it through the Spirit.

THIRST AFTER GOD

It is the hungry souls God feeds, and it is the thirsty ones on whom He pours His Spirit (Luke 1:53).

What do you desire in life more than anything else? Is it money, fame, pleasure—or do you thirst after God? Do you feel your greatest need is to know Him and be baptized with His Spirit? If that is how you really feel, you can receive the divine blessing to satisfy that desire.

The Psalmist cried, "My soul thirsteth for God, for the living God" (Psalm 42:2). His prayer was, "I stretch forth my hands unto thee: my soul thirsteth after thee, as a thirsty land" (Psalm 143:6). He knew how thirsty the land can be in dry weather. Water has always been a precious commodity in the Holy Land, and the Psalmist undoubtedly experienced times of drought when every living thing would suffer. Pasture would burn up; flocks perish; wildlife die; men and women famish. The situation would be desperate —and it was with a similar degree of spiritual desperation that he cried, "O God, thou art my God; early will I seek thee: my soul thirsteth for thee, my flesh longeth for thee in a dry and thirsty land, where no water is" (Psalm 119:174).

Is that the way you feel? Is your spirit parched? Do you long for God the way the desert longs for water? Do you thirst to the point of desperation? If you do, He will satisfy your thirst, for He has promised, "I will pour water upon him that is thirsty, and floods upon the dry ground: I will pour my spirit upon thy seed, and my blessing upon thine offspring" (Isaiah 44:3).

BE SURE YOUR MOTIVES ARE RIGHT

There are two basic conditions to be met: you must thirst, and you must pray. For God's promises are not self-executing. Though He offers to fill you with His Spirit, you cannot expect Him to do so unless you pray. Neither can you expect His blessing unless you are obedient.

We read in Acts 5:32 that God gives the Holy Ghost "to them that obey him," so if there is any way in which you may have disobeyed the Scriptures you should confess your sin, forsake it, and ask God's forgiveness.

Only when our hearts are free from condemnation can we ask in faith and receive the blessing. The Bible says, "Beloved, if our heart condemn us not, then have we confidence toward God. And whatsoever we ask, we receive of him, because we keep his commandments, and do those things that are pleasing in his sight" (1 John 3:21, 22).

It is possible to ask from a wrong motive. Do you want the experience for personal gain of some kind? Will it give you favor with certain people if you are baptized with the Holy Ghost? Is it the ecstasy of the Baptism that appeals to you? Do you want to be filled merely to enjoy an "emotional binge" that will make you "feel good"? If so, you will be disappointed.

Two incidents in Jacob's life teach a valuable lesson along this line. The first occurred at Beersheba, where Jacob played a trick and deceived his father into giving the paternal blessing to him instead of his brother (see Genesis 27:19). Jacob paid dearly for that ruse, for he himself was the victim of cruel deception time after time. Though he gained his father's blessing, he could not obtain God's blessing by trickery.

It was at Peniel Jacob received the blessing from heaven. It was there he wrestled with a heavenly being until he prevailed. "I will not let thee go, except thou bless me," he declared, and he struggled persistently until daybreak. At last, after a long night of wrestling, he obtained the heavenly blessing (Genesis 32:29).

LET NOTHING DISCOURAGE YOU

The Bible encourages us to be persistent like Jacob in claiming God's promise. Do you remember the story of the man who wakened his friend at midnight to borrow some bread? (Luke 11:5). The friend arose and granted his request simply because the man kept asking. The Lord Jesus told this story to illustrate what He meant when He said, "Ask, and it shall be given you; seek, and ye shall find; knock, and it shall be opened unto you." If you keep asking, seeking, and knocking long enough your request will be granted.

But those who stop praying, or who seek the blessing from a wrong motive, will be disappointed; for James 4:3 says, "Ye ask, and receive not, because ye ask amiss, that ye may consume it upon your lusts."

The Bible says, "Delight thyself also in the Lord; and he shall give thee the desires of thine heart" (Psalm 37:4). If your motive is simply to please the Lord, and if you refuse to be denied, your prayer will be answered.

Wait on the Lord; worship Him; meditate on His precious promises. Let your heart be going out to God in prayer continually, reminding Him of your desire, and keep expecting the answer.

Mingle praise with your prayer, and while asking for greater blessings do not forget to thank the Lord for the blessings you already have.

If a friend gave you a check, would you wait until you cashed it before thanking Him? You have God's promise. Thank Him, even now, that the promised Gift is yours—by faith. By thanksgiving and praise you will hasten the moment of your personal Baptism.

EXPECT THE FULLNESS OF THE BLESSING

Do not be satisfied with anything less than a genuine, life-changing Baptism. There are some who get only a taste and they try to convince themselves that they have the fullness. God wants to give you an experience that will leave no room for doubt or disappointment.

Some Christians are like the chameleon. This little lizard is capable of changing color to match its mood or surroundings. The change is one of appearance only; it is temporary, and only skin deep. Christians who fail to receive a genuine Baptism but try to believe they have are like that. When they worship with Spirit-filled people they act like them; they talk like them; they give the appearance of being Spirit-filled; but it is just a facade, and underneath they are still empty, hungry, and dissatisfied.

Don Mallough tells the story of a boy with a questioning mind who for a long time wondered what caused the wind to blow. After much reasoning he arrived at what he thought was a logical answer. He decided the wind was produced by the moving of the branches in the trees!

The idea is preposterous, but not any more so than the supposition some people have concerning the Baptism. Because the incoming of the Holy Spirit is accompanied by speaking with tongues, they suppose the speaking with tongues brings the Spirit. And because there are certain manifestations such as trembling or falling when God baptizes a person in the Spirit, they suppose that by shaking themselves or falling prostrate they can obtain the blessing. This is a sad mistake, for it robs them of a genuine experience.

In contrast to the chameleon, think of the caterpillar. It is a larva; it spins a cocoon and hibernates, during which time it experiences a complete change (a metamorphosis) and emerges as a beautiful butterfly or moth. The change is one of nature, as well as appearance. Whereas it was the nature of the larva to crawl, it is the nature of the butterfly to soar. God wishes to effect a metamorphosis in the Spirit-filled life. Through the Baptism He desires the timid one to become bold; the weak to become strong; the quiet to become vocal. The change can be deep and real when the Spirit dwells within.

KEEP LOOKING TO THE LORD

The blessing comes from heaven. The sound that was heard on the Day of Pentecost came from heaven (Acts 2:2), and the Spirit who came upon Jesus in the form of a dove descended from above (Matthew 3:16). Jesus, the One who baptizes with the Holy Ghost, is in heaven (Acts 2:33), so keep your heart and mind focused on Him while seeking the Baptism.

The Scriptures do not say very much about how we should receive—but they say a great deal about how the Lord will give. "He will pour out. . . ." "He will baptize. . . ." "He will send. . . ." "He will give. . . ."

The Bible presents the Baptism from the standpoint of the Giver, rather than the receiver, for a very good reason. It is to keep us from being introspective—to keep our thoughts directed toward the One who gave the promise.

Earnest prayer will not help unless it is properly directed. This is illustrated in the story of the epileptic's father, recorded in Luke 9:38-42. The father "besought" the disciples to cast the demon out of the afflicted boy, but they could not do so. Then he said to Jesus, "Master, I beseech thee, look upon my son. . . ." It was the same prayer (for "beseech" is from the same Greek word as "besought") but now it was directed toward Jesus, instead of the disciples, and therefore his prayer was answered.

The prophets of Baal were certainly as earnest in their prayer on Mount Carmel as Elijah was (1 Kings 18:26). In fact, they were desperate, and they prayed all day, from morning to evening; but it was Elijah's prayer, and not theirs, which brought the fire from heaven. The difference lay in the One to whom prayer was directed.

The reason some people do not receive the Baptism is that they keep their minds on themselves. They think of their feelings; they wonder if they have enough faith; they try one posture after another; they accuse themselves of being unworthy; when all the time God is holding the gift in His hands ready to bestow it on them as soon as they will reach out and take it. That is why the Bible emphasizes God's side of the Baptism instead of ours. He wants us to forget the receiver and look to the Giver.

Reach Out and Take the Gift

In Revelation 22:17 we read, "And the Spirit and the bride say, Come. And let him that heareth say, Come. And let him that is athirst come. And whosoever will, let him *take* the water of life freely." Arthur Graves has pointed out that this word *take* is the same Greek word that is translated "receive" in the references to receiving the Spirit. It means to reach out and take a gift that is extended. God gives the Spirit, but we must take it from His hand. This is the way we receive any gift from God.

John used this same word in speaking of Christ. He said that "as many as *received* him, to them gave he power to become the sons of God" (John 1:12).

Peter also used the word when he said that "whosoever believeth in him shall *receive* remission of sins" (Acts 10:43).

Paul used it when he said, "We also joy in God through our Lord Jesus Christ, by whom we have now *received* the atonement" (Romans 5:11).

Jesus used the same word when He said, "He that *taketh* not his cross, and followeth after me, is not worthy of me" (Matthew 10:38).

If you know how to receive Christ—if you know how to receive the atonement—how to take the water of life, and to take your cross, then you know how to receive the Holy Spirit. Just reach out in faith. You believe He will give it, for He promised—so you ask Him for it, fully convinced that He will grant your request.

Chapter Three

What Are the Immediate Evidences?

CONSIDER THE AMAZING CHANGES
that came over the disciples when they were
filled with the Spirit. Before Pentecost they
were unsure, unsteady, unfaithful. When Jesus was arrested and put on trial, they all
forsook Him and fled (Matthew 26:56); but
after Pentecost they immediately were brave
as lions, able to stand before their enemies
and proclaim the gospel in spite of bitter persecution (Acts 5:29).

POWER TO WITNESS FOR CHRIST

Jesus had said it would happen. Prior to
the Day of Pentecost He had told His disciples, "Ye shall receive power, after that the
Holy Ghost is come upon you: and ye shall
be witnesses unto me" (Acts 1:8). A better
translation is, "You shall receive power when
the Holy Spirit has come upon you; and you
shall be My witnesses" (New American Standard Bible).

"My witnesses," Jesus said. This is the prime
purpose of the Pentecostal enduement and a
prime evidence of the Baptism. Spirit-filled

people witness for Jesus. The Holy Ghost comes to testify of Jesus "and ye also shall bear witness, because ye have been with me from the beginning" (John 15:27). They had been eyewitnesses of His life, His works, His death and resurrection, but to make their personal testimony effective they would need the co-witness of the Holy Ghost.

VICTORY OVER EVERY SIN

Hudson Taylor said, "What is wanted is not that we should get more of the Spirit, but that the Spirit should get more of us." This is the secret of victorious Christian living, and we begin to learn it when we yield ourselves fully to God to be filled with the Spirit.

Without the Baptism we are likely to fight temptation in our own strength, and lose. When the Holy Ghost controls our lives, we find the sins that formerly tripped us have lost their power. "Sin shall not have dominion over you," Paul wrote (Romans 6:14). "They that are after the flesh do mind the things of the flesh; but they that are after the Spirit the things of the Spirit" (Romans 8:5).

Though we sometimes have battles, God will strengthen us with all might by His Spirit in the inner man, and flood our souls with the love of Christ until we are "filled with all the fullness of God" (Ephesians 3:13-20). What a privilege it is to be temples of the Holy Ghost. We are hosts and hostesses to Deity! If we are tempted with some trait of the flesh, the Spirit will help us to overcome. If we are tempted to feel guilty and condemned, we can turn a deaf ear to the accusations of Satan and know that there is "no condemnation to them that are in Christ Jesus, who walk not after the flesh, but after the Spirit" (Romans 8:1).

SPEAKING WITH TONGUES

One immediate and spectacular sign of being baptized with the Holy Ghost is "speaking with other tongues." The New Testament has much to say about this practice.

Jesus had said, "These signs shall follow them that believe . . . they shall speak with new tongues" (Mark 16:17). His words were fulfilled on the Day of Pentecost when the Holy Spirit fell on the 120 disciples in the upper room. For we read, "They were all filled with the Holy Ghost, and began to speak with other tongues, as the Spirit gave them utterance" (Acts 2:4).

These are tongues of supernatural utterance. The name given in the 19th century to this devout practice, and widely used today, is *glossolalia,* which simply means "tongues speaking" (from the Greek words *glossa,* meaning language, and *lalia,* meaning to speak).

Harold Horton explained "speaking with other tongues" as follows:

"It is the supernatural utterance by the Holy Spirit in languages never learned by the speaker, nor understood by the speaker, and nearly always not understood by the hearer. It has nothing whatever to do with linguistic ability, nor with the mind or intellect of man. It is a manifestation of the mind of the Spirit of God employing human speech organs. When a man is speaking with tongues, his mind, intellect, and understanding are quiet. It is the faculty of God that is active. Man's will certainly is active, and his spirit and his speech organs; but the mind that is operating is the mind of God through the Holy Spirit."

THE EVIDENCE AT SAMARIA

When the church at Jerusalem was broken up by persecution, Philip went to the city of Samaria and preached Christ there. His preaching met with a tremendous response. Many were converted and baptized in the name of the Lord Jesus, and there were mighty miracles of healing. Shortly afterwards Peter and John came to the city. They prayed for the converts, that they might receive the Holy Ghost, for He had not yet fallen on any of them, and Acts 8:17 tells us what happened: "Then laid they their hands on them, and they received the Holy Ghost."

There was a man named Simon in that church, who formerly had been a sorcerer. "And when Simon saw that through laying on of the apostles' hands the Holy Ghost was given, he offered them money, saying, Give me also this power, that on whomsoever I lay hands, he may receive the Holy Ghost." Of course, Peter rebuked the man for thinking he could buy spiritual power with money. The point we wish to make, however, is that

when the Samaritans received the Holy Ghost
something happened which was so evident
and so spectacular that this former sorcerer
wanted to learn how to make it happen.

There are churches today which teach the
Baptism is a quiet, inward work of God without any special outward evidence. If this were
true, would someone as shrewd as Simon have
offered money? Would he have wished to
practice the laying on of hands, if there had
been nothing he could see or hear? We are
persuaded that Simon saw and heard something that no sorcerer could imitate. We have
no doubt that the Samaritans spoke with other tongues when they were baptized with the
Holy Ghost, just as the 120 did on the Day
of Pentecost.

TONGUES SPOKEN AT CAESAREA

The next recorded instance of "speaking
with tongues" occurred at Caesarea.

Cornelius was a Roman officer. He and his
family were Gentiles, and up to this time no
Gentiles had been baptized with the Holy
Ghost; but the Lord led Peter to go to Caesarea and preach at this man's house; and
while Peter was preaching "the Holy Ghost
fell on all them which heard the word" (Acts
10:44).

Peter and his companions (Christian Jews)
were astonished to see the gift of the Holy
Ghost being poured out upon the Gentiles.
They thought the gift was only for Jews! But
when they saw what happened, they knew
these Gentiles had received the Holy Ghost,

"for they heard them speak with tongues, and magnify God" (Acts 10:46).

Peter returned to Jerusalem and told the other apostles how the Gentiles had received the Word and had been filled with the Spirit. The others could not believe it, at first, but Peter convinced them by saying, "As I began to speak, the Holy Ghost fell on them, as on us at the beginning" (Acts 11:15). In other words, the Gentiles at Caesarea experienced the same mighty Baptism as the 120 experienced at Jerusalem on the Day of Pentecost.

THE OUTPOURING AT EPHESUS

The outpouring of the Spirit at Ephesus has already been mentioned (Acts 19). This happened some 20 years after the initial outpouring on the Day of Pentecost.

Here again there was the initial physical evidence of speaking with other tongues, for we read: "And when Paul had laid his hands upon them, the Holy Ghost came on them: and they spake with tongues, and prophesied" (Acts 19:6).

PAUL'S PERSONAL EXPERIENCE

The personal experience of the apostle Paul should not be overlooked. He was not in the upper room when the Spirit fell, for he was not converted until some time later (Acts 9).

The Bible tells how Ananias put his hands on Paul and prayed for him that he might receive his sight and "be filled with the Holy Ghost" (Acts 9:17). Evidently the request of

Ananias was answered. Paul had been blind, but now he could see. If one part of the prayer was answered, it is safe to conclude that the other was also! Although the Scriptures do not state specifically that Paul spoke in tongues at this time, we know that he did have this experience, for he later wrote to the Christians at Corinth and said, "I thank my God, I speak with tongues more than ye all" (1 Corinthians 14:18).

THE VALUE OF TONGUES

Some may wonder why God chose this particular sign as an evidence of the Baptism. James 3:8 may give a clue. It says, "The tongue can no man tame; it is an unruly evil, full of deadly poison." Of all members of the human body, the tongue is the most difficult to subdue. If the tongue can be controlled, the whole body can be controlled.

Speaking with tongues is, in fact, the highest spiritual exercise of which a mortal man is capable. What exactly are its uses? Ian Macpherson has mentioned three:

First, tongues magnify the Lord. "We do hear them speak in our tongues the wonderful works of God" (Acts 2:11). "They heard them speak with tongues and magnify God" (Acts 10:46). "I will sing with the Spirit" (1 Corinthians 14:15). It is a blessed form of worship!

Second, tongues edify the believers. They edify the persons using them, whether privately or publicly. In addition, when coupled with the gift of interpretation they edify the hearers. "He that speaketh in a tongue edifieth himself" (1 Corinthians 14:4). "Let him that speaketh in a tongue pray that he may interpret, so that [he] may excel to the edifying of the church" (1 Corinthians 4:13, 12).

Third, tongues testify. "For with stammering lips and another tongue will he speak to this people" (Isaiah 28:11). "Every man heard them speak in his own language" (Acts 2:6). This does not mean, as is often supposed, that the early disciples were miraculously endowed with ability to understand and speak foreign languages without grammar lessons and diction studies. It is evident from Acts 14:11, 14 that neither Paul nor Barnabas understood the speech of the Lycaonians.

Surely, when tongues fulfill such vital functions, it is no marvel that Paul said, "Forbid not to speak with tongues" (1 Corinthians 14:39).

Chapter Four

What Are the Long-Range Benefits?

THE HOLY SPIRIT comes to abide, not merely to visit. Jesus said, "I will pray the Father, and he shall give you another Comforter, that he may *abide with you for ever;* even the Spirit of truth" (John 14:16, 17). The Baptism, therefore, is not a passing event but the beginning of a lifelong experience. It is not merely an episode but an epoch marking a new period of great spiritual development with the Holy Ghost resident within.

A SPIRIT-FILLED LIFE

The command, "Be filled with the Spirit" (Ephesians 5:18), signifies not only an initial filling but a constant inflow to keep us full of the Spirit. The Greek verb speaks of a continuing action. Literally it means, "Be getting filled with the Spirit." We are like an electric cord—useless unless plugged in. We are only conductors. We have no power when separated from the Source, which is God Himself.

This is the great, lasting benefit of the

Baptism—a Spirit-filled life of power, joy, and love. "The love of God is shed abroad in our hearts by the Holy Ghost which is given to us" (Romans 5:5). This divine love causes us to love others more than ourselves. It constrains us to exalt our Lord rather than ourselves. It makes us Christlike and wins the admiration of the world, proving that we are indeed the disciples of Jesus (John 13:35).

It is also a life of purity. We are "baptized with the Holy Ghost, and with fire" (Matthew 3:11), and the fire purges. It burns up the chaff (the straw) in our lives (Matthew 3:12; Luke 3:17). As a farmer at harvesttime threshes the grain and throws the straw in the fire, so the Holy Ghost separates the grain from the chaff, the good seed from the husks.

The Blood cleanses and the Fire purifies. It takes the blood of Jesus to make us clean and the Spirit's fire to keep us clean. No germs of sin can survive the holy fire. The flaming presence of the Third Person of the Holy Trinity in our lives keeps us purged from impure thoughts, unclean speech, and unholy deeds as we live after the Spirit and not after the flesh.

WALKING IN THE SPIRIT

Writing in Galatians 5:25, Paul said, "If we live in the Spirit, let us also walk in the Spirit." In other words, if we receive spiritual life through the Holy Spirit we should give our daily lives to the Spirit, and let Him lead us and use us for God's glory.

The "oil" of the Spirit gives us light. In Bible times, oil was the chief means of illumination at night. The five young women who were "foolish" ran out of oil and their lamps went out (Matthew 25:10). When we keep filled with the Holy Ghost our lights keep burning. We are saved from darkness and our light draws others to Christ.

The indwelling Spirit keeps us in peace. This is symbolized very beautifully by the dove at Jesus' baptism. John said, "I saw the Spirit descending from heaven like a dove, and it abode upon him" (John 1:32). Doves have no bitter gall. They are not birds of prey. They are peace-loving, and we too are peace-loving when filled with the Spirit.

The Spirit is also symbolized by water. Water sustains life. It satisfies thirst, and so does the Holy Ghost. Jesus said, "If any man thirst, let him come unto me, and drink" (John 7:37). We need to accept His invitation and keep drinking of the Spirit. The supply we receive when we are baptized with the Holy Ghost does not last forever. We need to drink each day in order to keep filled with the Spirit.

FRUIT OF THE SPIRIT

When filled with the Spirit we can bear the fruit of the Spirit. This long-range benefit of the Baptism is basic in the Christian life and supremely important.

"The fruit of the Spirit is love, joy, peace, long-suffering, gentleness, goodness, faith, meekness, temperance" (Galatians 5:22, 23).

Someone has divided these nine "fruits" into clusters of three, as follows.

"Love, joy, peace" are qualities which particularly affect our relationship to God. We love Him. We joy in Him. We are at peace with Him.

"Long-suffering, gentleness, goodness" speak of Christlike attitudes toward others. We are patient toward everyone. We treat them gently. We are good to them.

"Faith, meekness, temperance" are inward characteristics which the Spirit develops in our lives. We become marked by faithfulness, loyalty, and dependability. We are meek, not self-willed. We are disciplined and temperate, not extremists.

The Scriptures have much to say about these nine qualities called "the fruit of the Spirit." It all may be summed up in one word—Christlikeness; for the work of the Holy Ghost is to make us like our Lord Jesus always and in every respect.

COMFORT OF THE SPIRIT

We have quoted John 14:16 where Jesus spoke of the Holy Spirit as the Comforter. This word had a stronger meaning in days gone by than it has today. It meant "One who strengthens and invigorates."

The word "Comforter" is from *Parakletos,* a Greek word which means "called alongside" (from the Greek words *para,* meaning "to the side of," and *kaleo,* "to summon"). It was a technical term used in Greek courts of justice. It referred to an advocate, one who pleads the cause of another, one who is called to another's side to aid him.

A missionary among the Karre people in Africa found it very difficult to translate "Comforter" into their language. She could find no comparable word, so she questioned one African after another. Carefully she explained that the Holy Ghost encourages, admonishes, protects, helps, strengthens, comforts, and guides the Christian.

"Isn't there some word that has this meaning?" she asked. They all shook their heads. She was at the point of frustration when finally someone said, "If someone would do all that for us, we would say, 'He falls down beside us.'" He explained that porters in Africa go on very long journeys carrying heavy loads on their heads. If they grow exhausted they may collapse along the lonely trail. One may lie there all night, sick and helpless, in danger of being eaten by wild animals. However, if he is fortunate someone may come along the trail, find him, and take pity on him. This friend, like the Good Samaritan, may stoop down, pick the porter up, and carry him to safety in the next village. The Karre people refer to such a good person as "The one who falls down beside us." That was the very term the missionary wanted; it expressed just what the Comforter does for the Christian believer.

GIFTS OF THE SPIRIT

Another great benefit of being baptized with the Holy Ghost is to receive spiritual gifts. As pointed out in 1 Corinthians 12:27, the Church is the body of Christ and we are members of that body. Just as the human body is animated by one spirit, the body of Christ, which is the Church, is energized by the Holy Spirit, and gifted with spiritual enablements with which to function.

These enablements are *spiritual* gifts, not natural gifts. Each of us has natural gifts, such as sight, hearing, singing, oratory, or leadership, but these should not be confused with the supernatural gifts of the Holy Spirit.

Sometimes God chooses the most unlikely persons on whom to bestow His spiritual gifts. He may endow the most timid, reticent individual with a mighty gift of utterance in the Spirit, and He may impart the gift of the word of wisdom to the most unlearned person imagineable. The Lord loves to choose "the foolish things of the world to confound the wise; and God hath chosen the weak things of the world to confound the things which are mighty; and base things of the world, and things which are despised. . . . That no flesh should glory in his presence" (1 Corinthians 1:27-29).

GIFTS OF REVELATION

There are nine gifts listed in 1 Corinthians 12:8-10 and these may be divided in three groups. "The word of wisdom," "the word of knowledge," and "the discerning of spirits" may be classified as gifts of revelation.

Stephen had the gift of the *word of wisdom;* it was evident both in his preaching (Acts 6:

10) and in his defense before the council (Acts 7). James also exercised this gift in settling the dispute concerning the Gentiles (Acts 15:19).

There is an infinite reservoir of knowledge hidden in the Lord (Colossians 2:3) and He releases small portions through the gift of *"the word of knowledge."* Notice how the language indicates the limited extent of the revelation: it is merely a *word* of knowledge —but it is given just when needed according to God's all-wise plan.

The gift of *discerning of spirits* that motivate people is another great blessing to the Church. When Philip went to Samaria and preached the gospel, one of his converts was Simon the sorcerer. Evidently Philip did not have the gift of discerning of spirits, or he would not have been fooled by the sorcerer's profession of faith; but when Peter came he discerned that Simon was motivated by an evil spirit (Acts 8:21).

GIFTS OF POWER

The fourth gift mentioned in 1 Corinthians 12 is the *gift of faith*. This is not merely a saving faith which is given to us at conversion; it is the faith Jesus mentioned in Matthew 17:20 when He said, "If ye have faith as a grain of mustard seed, ye shall say unto this mountain, Remove hence to yonder place; and it shall remove; and nothing shall be impossible unto you." Paul mentioned this in 1 Corinthians 13:2 saying, "And though I have all faith, so that I could remove mountains. . . ." Paul exercised this gift of faith when he spoke the word of authority at Lystra, in the healing of the lame man (Acts 14:10), and again at Troas, in bringing Eutychus back to life (Acts 20:10).

The gift of the *working of miracles* also was seen in Paul's ministry. There were "special miracles" through cloths taken from his body (Acts 19:11, 12). Stephen had this gift, for he was "full of power" (Acts 6:8). Peter had it too, as manifested in the healing of palsied Aeneas and the restoration of Dorcas who had died (Acts 9:32-42).

Then there are the *gifts of healings.* God has set these gifts in the Church and there are many illustrations of their operation in the Book of Acts. The laying on of hands (Mark 16:17, 18) and the anointing with oil (James 5:14, 15) are two ways in which these gifts of healings operate.

GIFTS OF UTTERANCE

The gift of *prophecy* comes first in this group and it is given top place among all the gifts. We are told to especially covet this gift (1 Corinthians 14:1, 39), the reason being that this gift is the medium by which all the other gifts find expression. Prophesying may include *foretelling* or it may be limited to *forthtelling* if God sees fit. It means to speak for God. When an event is *foretold* through a Spirit-given utterance it should not be considered infallible. The apostle says that when the prophets have spoken, others are to "judge" or "discern" to decide whether the prophecy is from the Lord. It is possible for the human spirit to enter into an inspired utterance and to color (or discolor) it. The Scripture therefore places strict limits upon the use of the gift of prophecy. It stipulates that prophecy is given to edify, exhort, and comfort the Church (1 Corinthians 14:3).

With reference to the *gift of tongues*, the apostle said the chief use of this gift is for prayer (1 Corinthians 14:14). When the Holy Spirit prays through us in tongues, He is able to pray according to the will of God (Romans 8:26). He who speaks in an unknown tongue edifies himself (1 Corinthians 14:4) and that is good. However, if the utterance in tongues is followed by an interpretation so that the hearers will understand the message, the Church is edified, and that is even better (1 Corinthians 14:16). Therefore the *gift of interpretation of tongues* is needed in the body of Christ.

In addition to the nine gifts already mentioned, there are gifts of *ministry,* of *giving,* of *ruling,* etc. See Romans 12:6-8.

FILLED AND REFILLED

There is one Baptism and many refillings. Peter was baptized with the Holy Ghost on the Day of Pentecost (Acts 2:4) but a short time later he was again "filled with the Holy Ghost" (Acts 4:8). This was when he was addressing the Jewish leaders who had arrested him.

Following the apostles' arrest and release, there was a general prayer meeting of the believers. They prayed that God would give them greater boldness to preach the Word.

"And when they had prayed, the place was shaken where they were assemblied together; and they were all filled with the Holy Ghost, and they spake the word of God with boldness" (Acts 4:31). They had been baptized with the Holy Ghost earlier, but now they were refilled.

God refills us again and again because He wants us to be like streams, not ponds. A pond may be formed overnight by a single rainstorm. It fills quickly, serves a useful purpose for a while, but gradually loses its water to the sun and soil; then one hot day the thirsty cattle come to drink and all they find is a crust of mud.

Some Christians have an experience like that. A revival comes to the community and they are filled with the Holy Ghost, but after a while they "dry up" and in place of the pure water of the Spirit that came from heaven there is nothing left but the hard "mud" of the old human nature.

So we need not just one infilling, but many. One rainstorm makes a pond, but repeated rains make a river. Jesus said that if we believe on Him, the Spirit will fill us and flow from our innermost being like "rivers of living water."

Each time a new challenge faces us, we can receive a new filling to meet it. Each time we go before a Sunday school class to teach, or deal with someone concerning Christ, we can be refilled. At the beginning of each new day we can be filled anew with the Holy Spirit. In this way we can fulfill the command, "Be filled with the Spirit," so that our lives constantly may bring blessing to others and glory to God.

The Gifts of the Spirit
1934 - Harold Horton